Engineered!
Engineering Design at Work

Shannon Hunt

James Gulliver Hancock

Kids Can Press

To Dave, for the rings — one gold, one iron — and everything they bring,
and to Casey and Remy for making my heart happy every day — S.H.

For my little engineer, Quinn. May you find out how everything works. — J.G.H.

Acknowledgments

Special thanks for their time and expertise to Mark Ellens, P.Eng.; Jon Holland, P.E. (Brown and Caldwell); Dr. Danielle Marceau (Schulich School of Engineering, University of Calgary); Arianna McAllister; Sean McDermott (Cervélo); Sarah Taylor (Cervélo).

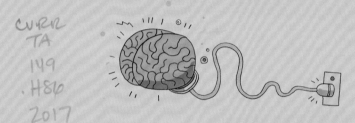

Text © 2017 Shannon Hunt
Illustrations © 2017 James Gulliver Hancock

Kids Can Press gratefully acknowledges the financial support of the Government of Ontario, through the Ontario Media Development Corporation; the Ontario Arts Council; the Canada Council for the Arts; and the Government of Canada, through the CBF, for our publishing activity.

Published in Canada and the U.S. by Kids Can Press Ltd.
25 Dockside Drive, Toronto, ON M5A 0B5

Kids Can Press is a Corus Entertainment Inc. company

www.kidscanpress.com

The artwork in this book was rendered in pencil on paper and colored in Photoshop.
The text is set in Picadilly.

Photo credits:
Page 12: NASA / JPL-Caltech / Malin Space Science Systems
Page 25: Corbis Historical / Getty Images
Page 33: Reuters
Page 37: Yann Arthus-Bertrand / Getty Images
Page 44: Earl Wilson of Brown and Caldwell

Edited by Yasemin Uçar and Katie Scott
Designed by Marie Bartholomew

Printed and bound in Shenzhen, China, in 3/2017 by C&C Offset

CM 17 0 9 8 7 6 5 4 3 2 1

Library and Archives Canada Cataloguing in Publication

Hunt, Shannon (Shannon Chantal), author
  Engineered! : engineering design at work / written by Shannon Hunt ; illustrated by James Gulliver Hancock.

Includes index.
ISBN 978-1-77138-560-2 (hardback)

1. Engineering — Juvenile literature. 2. Engineering — Vocational guidance — Juvenile literature. 3. Engineers — Juvenile literature. I. Hancock, James Gulliver, illustrator II. Title

TA149.H86 2017   j620   C2016-906425-5

Contents

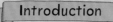

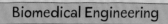
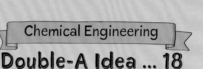
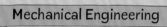
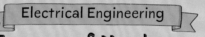
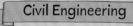
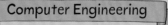
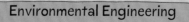

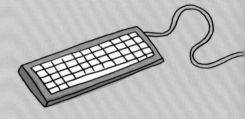
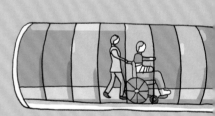

In the Minds of Engineers

It was late — 1:30 in the morning. Way past bedtime for most of us. But that didn't stop hundreds of people from gathering in New York City's Times Square on August 6, 2012. They were there to watch NASA's live coverage of an interplanetary drama unfolding on a massive five-story television screen. The star of the show wasn't a little green alien, but a car-sized silver rover called *Curiosity*.

After an eight-month voyage through space, it all came down to seven minutes: the time it would take to deposit *Curiosity* on the surface of Mars. Nail-biting gave way to high-fiving as the rover touched down safely. The historic landing was over in minutes, but the technology that made it possible had originated years before, in the minds of engineers.

Want to find out how engineers got *Curiosity* to Mars? You can read more about the mission on pages 8–13!

4

Who Are Engineers?

Engineers are problem solvers. They use their math, science and technology skills to find creative solutions to problems, such as landing *Curiosity* safely on the surface of Mars.

To solve these problems, engineers might improve existing technology. They might design a battery that lasts longer or build a bridge that can withstand a major earthquake. If existing technology won't solve the problem, engineers create new technology, such as a machine that prints skin substitutes for burn victims. Engineers design not only those batteries, bridges or printers, but also the machines, electronics and software to build them. Whatever the problem, engineers find creative and cost-effective solutions that work well.

Kids are natural engineers. You ask lots of questions, you're creative and you're good at solving problems, whether it's designing an alarm to keep your annoying brother out of your room or figuring out a way to make sure you — not your sister — get the biggest serving of *[insert your favorite food here]*.

CURIOSITY ON MARS

Engineering Design: Step-by-Step

Define   Investigate   Develop   Create   Test   Optimize   Share

When you have a problem to tackle — say, a messy room, a tricky math question or (*gasp!*) nothing to eat for dessert — you probably follow a step-by-step process until you arrive at a solution. When engineers are faced with a problem, they also follow a series of steps. They start by making sure they really understand the problem and, over time, they compare possible solutions, choose the best one, build working models and perfect the design.

Unlike following your favorite dessert recipe from start to finish, though, these design steps don't always happen in a fixed order. Sometimes good problem-solving means knowing when to go back to an earlier step and make a change, or even when to start over with a new idea.

Here's a look at how the engineering design process works.

1. Define the Problem

What needs to change?

At the start of a project, engineers identify the problem they are trying to solve, or the situation that needs to change.

2. Investigate Requirements

What are the criteria and constraints?

Engineers need to know the project's requirements. They identify the *criteria* (what people need and want from a solution) and the *constraints* (the restrictions or limitations they have to work within). Constraints might include how much money they can spend, safety standards to meet and when the project needs to be finished.

3. Develop and Compare Solutions

What is the best idea?

Next, engineers research and brainstorm possible solutions. This involves a lot of creativity and might even involve thinking of new technology that doesn't yet exist! Then the engineering team compares their ideas. They choose the one that is the best fit for the project's criteria and constraints.

4. Create

What will it look like?

Designing and building a working model, or *prototype*, allows engineers to see if their idea will work in the real world. The prototype is not always the same size as the finished product, and sometimes it is built with different materials.

Back to the drawing board!

6. Optimize

Can it be even better?

The prototype is improved, or optimized, to make it the best it can possibly be. Can it go faster? Can it be built using less expensive materials? Sometimes, optimizing means going back to an earlier stage to develop new solutions.

5. Test and Fix

Does it work?

The prototype is tested and retested to make sure it works and can withstand conditions in the real world. Anything that doesn't work gets fixed.

We did it!

7. Share Ideas

Who can we tell?

Finally, it's time to share the design with others outside the engineering team. That's how the solution to the problem becomes a reality!

Now you know the basics of engineering design. Turn the page to see how real engineers used these steps to solve *real* problems. Let's go engineer!

Seven Minutes of Terror

Have you ever been on a road trip? How long does it take for someone (yes, you!) to start asking, "Are we there yet?" Next time you're trapped in a moving car — with snacks, drinks and movie options running low — think of the spacecraft from NASA's *Mars Science Laboratory (MSL)*.

It survived the ultimate eight-month trip. From its launchpad in Cape Canaveral, Florida, the MSL spacecraft traveled 570 million kilometers (354 million miles) to its final destination: Gale Crater on Mars. Impressive, but getting to the Red Planet was only the beginning.

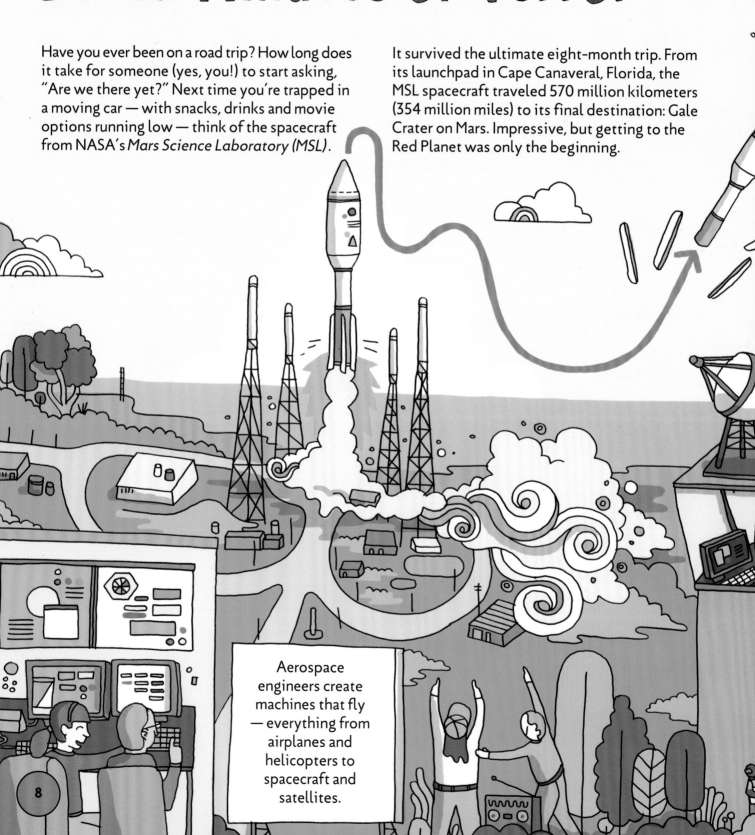

Aerospace engineers create machines that fly — everything from airplanes and helicopters to spacecraft and satellites.

8

An Epic Assignment

In August 2012, after surviving the epic voyage through space, the MSL spacecraft entered Mars's atmosphere and immediately faced an even greater challenge: landing its precious cargo safely on the planet's surface. Tucked inside the spacecraft was *Curiosity*, a modest-sized rover with a supersized assignment. Its mission: to search for evidence that the Gale Crater area could be — or was — a habitat for life on Mars.

Before *Curiosity* could start exploring the planet, it had to land. That meant slamming on the brakes big-time, slowing from about 21 243 km/h (13 200 m.p.h.) to about 2.7 km/h (1.7 m.p.h.). Think of going from supersonic speed to walking speed. The time it would take to do this is what NASA engineers called the "seven minutes of terror." Those seven minutes would decide *Curiosity*'s fate: would it crash and burn, or land and learn?

The assignment to make those seven minutes a success had started almost a decade earlier with the problem of how to create a landing system that would safely deposit *Curiosity* on the surface of Mars ❶.

Are we there yet?

When you see icons like this in the text, look for the Key Design Step box. The icons highlight the engineering design steps from pages 6–7.

Clara Ma, a sixth-grader from Kansas, won the contest to name the MSL rover. In her essay, Clara wrote, "Curiosity is the passion that drives us through our everyday lives ... We will never know everything there is to know, but with our burning curiosity, we have learned so much."

KEY DESIGN STEP

❶ **Define**

The Wrong Stuff

NASA engineers quickly started making a list of possible solutions — and then just as quickly rejected them.

One of the landing systems they considered was airbags, but not the kind you find in a car . These airbags would have to be strong enough to protect the spacecraft that housed *Curiosity* as it hit Mars's surface at high speed and then bounced to a stop.

Sounds sketchy, but this technology was tried and true: NASA had successfully used airbags to cocoon the landers carrying the skateboard-sized *Sojourner* rover and the coffee-table-sized *Spirit* and *Opportunity* rovers. Vectran, the fabric used to make those airbags, is almost twice as strong as the material used to make bulletproof vests. But there was one big problem with the airbag option — and that was *Curiosity* itself.

Curiosity would be loaded with scientific equipment: cameras, drills, a mass spectrometer to identify chemicals, and even a laser to vaporize rocks! All this equipment would make *Curiosity* weigh a ton ... literally! It would be the heaviest rover NASA had ever sent to Mars, and its landing system would have to support the rover's extreme weight. Airbags were not going to work. No fabric would be strong enough, not even Vectran, to make airbags that would survive bringing *Curiosity* in for a bouncy landing. The airbags would simply shred, and *Curiosity*'s mission would be over before it started.

If airbags wouldn't work, maybe legs would. NASA's *Viking* and *Phoenix* landers had used legs to safely touch down on the planet. Although simple and reliable, legs can also be tippy, especially when the lander carries a rover the size of *Curiosity*. Land on a slope, and the whole thing might topple over and be stranded like a helpless metallic beetle on its back.

> Airbags are quite cozy.

> Help me!

Even if the spacecraft arrived safely on the surface, Mars's terrain could make it challenging to get the ramps down and the rover out. What if steep slopes or inconveniently placed rocks stopped the ramps from opening? When *Sojourner* landed, the spacecraft's own airbags had temporarily blocked a ramp. MSL engineers knew that landing on Mars and then not being able to get *Curiosity* on the ground would be a billion-dollar boo-boo — costly and embarrassing!

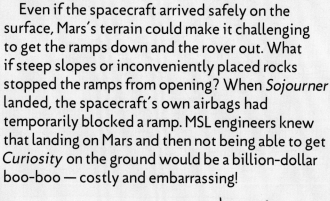

Rover on a Rope

NASA engineers were faced with a realization: they couldn't make these ideas work. To solve their landing dilemma, they needed a new solution — something that had never been done before. So they went back to the drawing board. One massive, multiday brainstorming session later, they came up with the kernel of an idea that would eventually solve their problem: the *Sky Crane maneuver* 💡.

The Sky Crane maneuver would be the final step in the landing sequence and would essentially lower *Curiosity* on nylon tethers, or ropes, to place it directly on the surface of Mars — similar to something you might see at a construction site.

The names of 1.24 million people who participated in NASA's Send Your Name to Mars program are etched into dime-sized silicon chips mounted onto *Curiosity*'s deck.

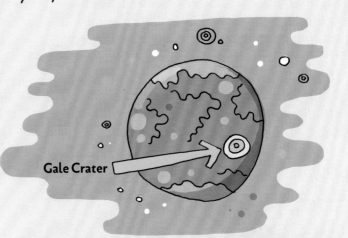

Gale Crater

SHAKE AND BAKE

Engineers can test their designs by building working models, or prototypes ⚙. They put these prototypes through trials, often under extreme conditions ✔. For the MSL mission, NASA engineers built two rovers: *Curiosity* and a stunt double. To make sure *Curiosity* could survive launch conditions, the rover was shaken as if it was in a major earthquake! The rover was also put into a chamber in which conditions on Mars could be simulated. The rover survived baking heat up to 40°C (104°F) and chilling cold down to −130°C (−202°F), more than enough to withstand the temperatures expected near *Curiosity*'s landing site on Mars. Now that's extreme!

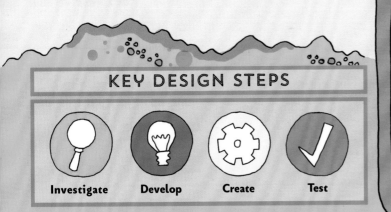

KEY DESIGN STEPS

Investigate   Develop   Create   Test

Putting On the Brakes

The Sky Crane maneuver was only the final part of the complicated entry, descent and landing sequence, which added up to those "seven minutes of terror." Remember, when the spacecraft entered Mars's atmosphere, it was streaking along at supersonic speed. Slowing it down required a series of *Mission Impossible*–type moves, including using the largest parachute NASA had ever designed. (During tests on Earth, the parachute barely fit in the world's largest wind tunnel!)

After the heat shield that protected the rover fell away, the spacecraft's backshell and parachute also separated. The spacecraft was reduced to a fancy jet backpack, called the descent stage, strapped to *Curiosity*. Guided by steerable rocket engines, the descent stage continued to slow *Curiosity*'s landing.

Spacecraft approaches Mars's atmosphere.

Cruise stage separates.

Parachute deploys and slows down the spacecraft.

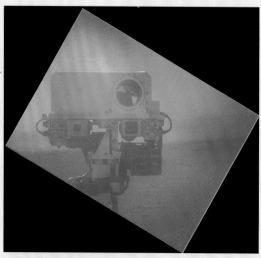

It's not all roving and rock sampling for Curiosity. The rover took time out to use a camera on its arm to snap this self-portrait — the first selfie on Mars!

• •
The science gleaned from the MSL mission might be priceless, but the mission itself had a price tag of $2.5 billion.

Mission Possible

About 15 seconds before touchdown, the Sky Crane maneuver got under way. *Curiosity* was lowered out of the descent stage on three nylon tethers. As the tethers and a cable supplying power unreeled, *Curiosity* was safely lowered to the surface, landing wheels first and ready to go — no tippy legs, no shredded airbags. Then, the descent stage released itself and flew away, leaving *Curiosity* safely on the surface of Mars.

"It looks a little bit crazy," acknowledged NASA engineer Adam Steltzner. "I promise you, it is the least crazy of the methods you could use to land a rover the size of *Curiosity* on Mars." Adam called the landing "the result of reasoned engineering thought."

On Mars, the billowing red, iron oxide–rich dust slowly settled. The minutes ticked by, and radio signals from *Curiosity* finally made their way back to Earth. At NASA's mission control, engineer Allen Chen broke the tense silence: "Touchdown confirmed. We're safe on Mars." Cheering, crying, clapping and high-fiving erupted. *Curiosity* had landed!

Oh, and just in case you're burning with some curiosity of your own, in March 2013, NASA announced that the analysis of a rock sample collected by *Curiosity* showed that in the past, Mars could have supported living microbes. Mission accomplished!

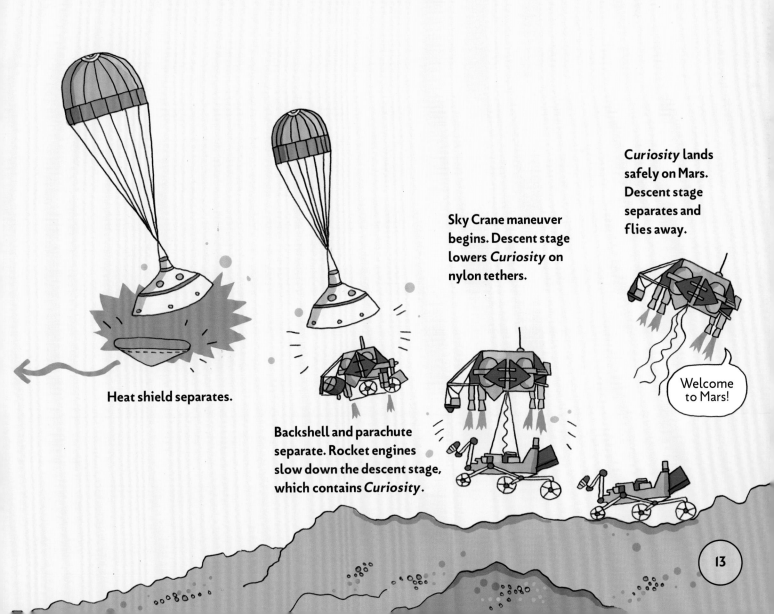

Heat shield separates.

Backshell and parachute separate. Rocket engines slow down the descent stage, which contains *Curiosity*.

Sky Crane maneuver begins. Descent stage lowers *Curiosity* on nylon tethers.

***Curiosity* lands safely on Mars. Descent stage separates and flies away.**

Welcome to Mars!

The Ultimate Print Job

Sometimes, getting a printer to spit out something — anything — is a mission in itself. And the chances of paper jams and empty ink cartridges seem to skyrocket when you have a big project due the next day. Some of today's printers are moving way past paper and ink, though. A new generation of 3D printers can make a mind-warping assortment of three-dimensional creations: superhero action figures, musical instruments, chess sets, cars (model- and life-sized!), clothing and even skin. Wait — *skin*? Yes, skin! A team of engineering students and professors at the University of Toronto (U of T) developed a special 3D printer that can do just that.

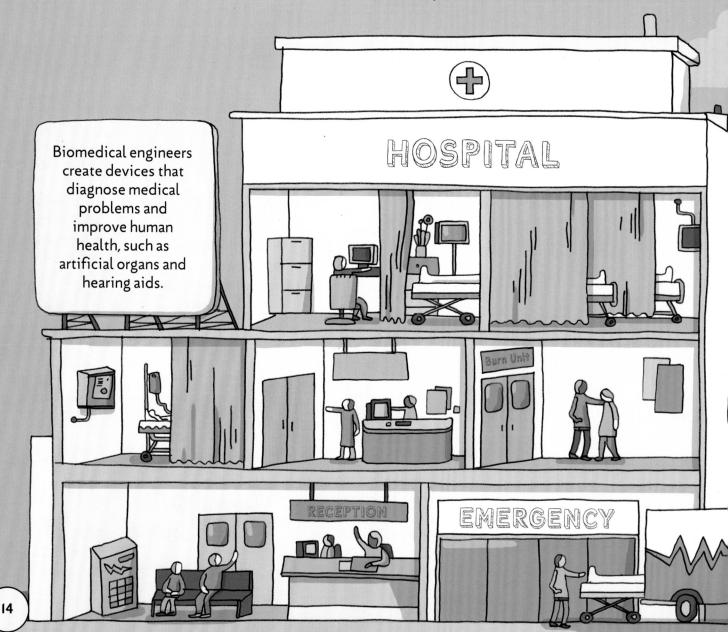

Biomedical engineers create devices that diagnose medical problems and improve human health, such as artificial organs and hearing aids.

Skin Deep

Your skin covers and protects you — it's your body's largest organ. When skin is badly damaged (from a deep wound or a bad burn, for example), it can have trouble healing, and that's seriously bad news ❗.

Doctors have several tricks in their medical bags to treat burn patients, but these treatment options aren't perfect. The most common treatment is grafting, or transplanting, healthy skin from other parts of the patient's body. *Ouch!* Grafting is not only painful, it's not even possible when patients have been burned over large parts of their bodies and don't have enough healthy tissue to graft.

Skin grafts from a donor are another option, but donor grafts can sometimes transmit bacteria and viruses, and even healthy grafts can be rejected by the patient's immune system. Doctors can also use skin substitutes, which are often made of synthetic material, but they are expensive and usually only available in well-equipped burn-care centers.

Because of these challenges, researchers are developing ways to create human tissue replacements in labs. "There is a constant need for replacement skin tissues when people have large or persistent wounds, burns and other skin lacerations," explains Arianna McAllister, one of the U of T team members. She says that's because "skin tissue can increase the rate of healing and reduce scarring." This need for skin tissue spurred Arianna and the rest of the U of T team to build their 3D printer.

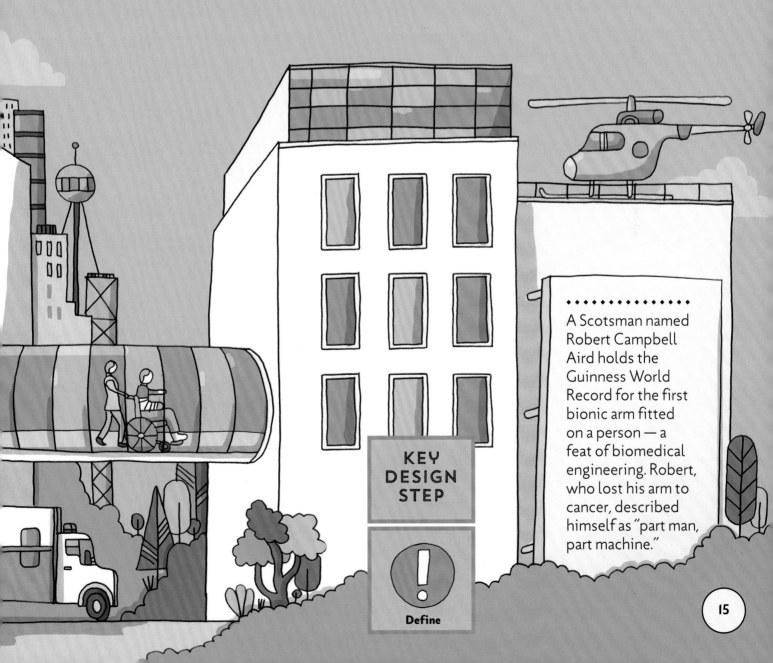

KEY DESIGN STEP

❗

Define

A Scotsman named Robert Campbell Aird holds the Guinness World Record for the first bionic arm fitted on a person — a feat of biomedical engineering. Robert, who lost his arm to cancer, described himself as "part man, part machine."

When Arianna McAllister, a team member on the 3D bioprinter, was young, she loved to take things apart and put them back together. It's no wonder she became an engineer, a job that allows her to design and build cool things every day! But for Arianna, engineering isn't just about creativity. Biomedical engineering, she says, allows you to have "a direct impact on people's lives, by reducing treatment time or complications." She says that at the end of the day, building something that can increase someone's quality of life is the coolest thing of all.

A Living Bandage

The team's *bioprinter* creates an artificial skin graft that is similar to real human skin. It is an improvement over current technology because it's less expensive, uses the patient's own skin cells (which eliminates the chance of rejection) and creates skin grafts fast — more than 200 square centimeters (31 square inches) per minute!

The bioprinter uses a special type of cartridge. Instead of holding ink like a regular printer, the cartridge contains the patient's skin cells! Inside the printer, a cell-filled solution is injected into a gel, which, when mixed with another solution, hardens and is shaped into long, soft gel sheets of artificial skin. The sheets are collected on a rotating drum, like plastic wrap on a roll, and can be printed in

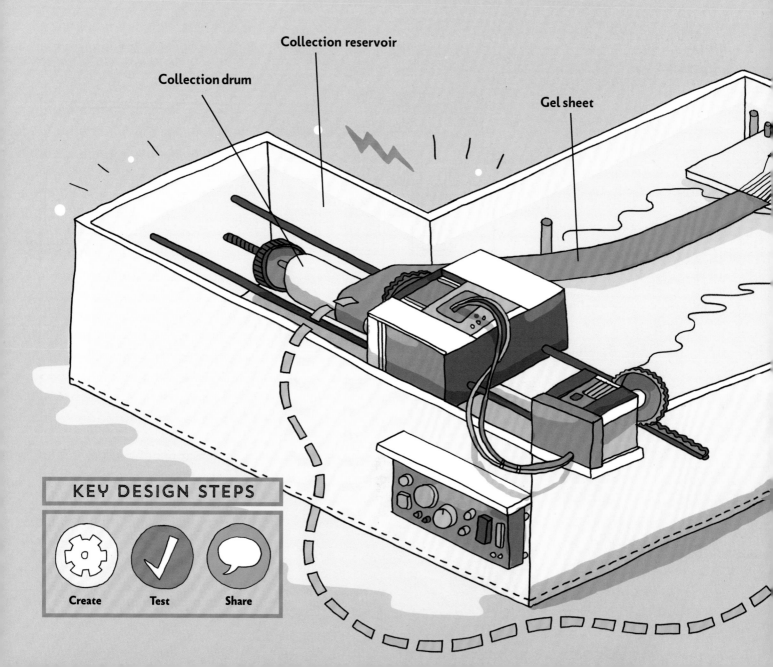

Collection reservoir

Collection drum

Gel sheet

KEY DESIGN STEPS

Create **Test** **Share**

many patterns — horizontal or vertical stripes, spots and holes (like Swiss cheese). The skin graft's thickness, structure and makeup can be controlled, so the graft is like a living bandage made to order.

Developing the bioprinter took years — testing hundreds of cartridge designs, combinations of materials and conditions for growing the cells ✔. But the hard work is paying off, and the team received funding to work with a children's hospital in Cambodia to help treat kids with burns. Arianna and the rest of the team are keen to tell others about their bioprinter, since it could revolutionize burn treatment around the world by offering an affordable solution ⬡. Now that sounds like the ultimate print job!

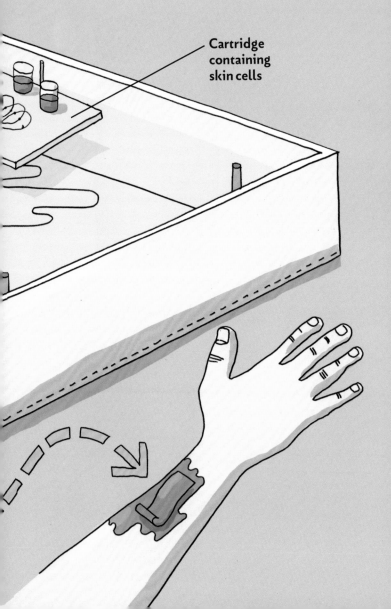

Cartridge containing skin cells

AN INVENTION THAT SUCKS

Englishman James Dyson made a name for himself with an invention that sucked — sucked up dust, pet hair and other unmentionables, that is. His famous bagless vacuum cleaner was the result of over 15 years of work and 5127 prototypes ⊙!

Today, James's charity sponsors the Dyson Award, an international award that challenges students to design something that solves a problem. That's exactly what Arianna and the team at U of T did. In fact, their bioprinter was the 2014 award-winning entry for Canada.

Double-A Idea

If the Energizer Bunny were beating his drum using batteries from the early 1950s, he would not keep going and going. The standard battery back then was the carbon-zinc battery, which didn't last long. That was a big problem for the company that made Eveready batteries. So in 1955,

they challenged one of their workers, chemical engineer Lewis Urry, to find a way to make their batteries last longer. Lewis eventually came up with a great idea — he just had to sell it to his boss, and he was going to use toy cars to help him do it.

Chemical engineers create ways to turn chemicals into many of the products we use every day, such as toothpaste, batteries, the rubber in sneakers and even certain foods!

Eveready later became Energizer. Their mascot, the Energizer Bunny, has been featured in over 100 television commercials and inspired a hot "hare" balloon taller than the Statue of Liberty. The term even made it into the dictionary as meaning "a persistent or indefatigable person or phenomenon."

KEY DESIGN STEPS

Develop   Share

Dead End

To understand Lewis's challenge, it helps to know how batteries work. Batteries don't store electricity — they create it through chemical reactions. Batteries have a cathode (a positive electrode) and an anode (a negative electrode). A substance called an electrolyte allows an electrical charge to flow between the cathode and anode, generating electricity.

The carbon-zinc battery used a mixture of powdered carbon and manganese dioxide for the cathode, zinc for the anode and a slightly acidic solution for the electrolyte. Lewis tried to make these batteries last longer, but he kept hitting dead ends. Eventually, he decided that the carbon-zinc battery wasn't part of the solution for a longer-lasting battery.

Lightning Volt

Lewis started experimenting with different combinations of substances to create a new kind of battery. One of these combinations — manganese dioxide for the cathode, zinc for the anode and an alkaline (the opposite of acidic) substance called potassium hydroxide for the electrolyte — was promising 💡. While he had created a battery that lasted longer, it wasn't generating enough power. After a lightning volt, uh, bolt, of inspiration, Lewis tried using powdered zinc instead of solid zinc as the anode. Eureka! Lewis had created a battery with more power and a longer life.

Lewis's new battery — the ancestor of some of the batteries rolling around your house today — was called an *alkaline battery*, after the alkaline electrolyte. It could outperform a carbon-zinc battery, but Lewis's good idea was as good as dead unless his boss could be sold on it.

Like his batteries, Lewis Urry just kept going and going. In his 77 years, he held over 50 patents, worked for the same company for 54 years and retired only a few months before his death.

Power Play

Lewis knew that a demonstration was worth a thousand words, so he bought two battery-operated toy cars on his way to work.

Lewis put a carbon-zinc battery in one toy car and his new alkaline battery in the other, and then invited his boss and coworkers to watch the show ⭕. It wasn't long before the car running on the carbon-zinc battery rolled to a stop. But the car powered by Lewis's alkaline battery ran so long that people got bored and went back to work! The new battery electrified Eveready, and by 1959, their alkaline batteries were selling in stores.

Consumers were sold, too, and over the years, new kinds of batteries, such as the lithium-ion battery used in cell phones, were developed to keep up with the consumer demand for portable devices. Think about it: without affordable, long-lasting batteries, people would still be carrying quarters for pay phones. In our book, Lewis gets an A — or a double A!

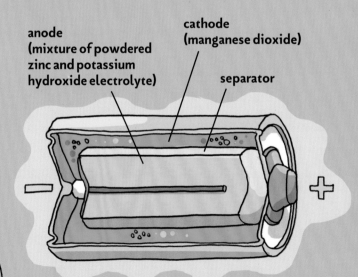

anode (mixture of powdered zinc and potassium hydroxide electrolyte)

cathode (manganese dioxide)

separator

An alkaline battery starts with a simple steel can exterior. Inside are a powdered zinc anode, a manganese dioxide mixture for the cathode and a separator to keep them apart.

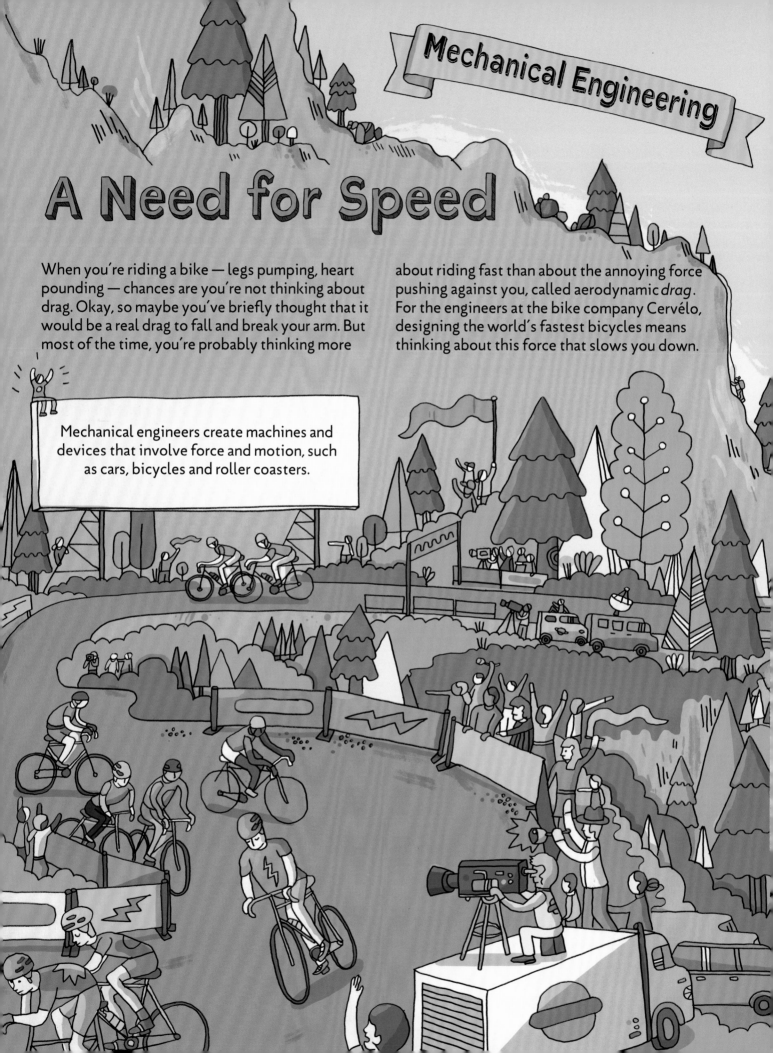

A Need for Speed

When you're riding a bike — legs pumping, heart pounding — chances are you're not thinking about drag. Okay, so maybe you've briefly thought that it would be a real drag to fall and break your arm. But most of the time, you're probably thinking more about riding fast than about the annoying force pushing against you, called aerodynamic *drag*. For the engineers at the bike company Cervélo, designing the world's fastest bicycles means thinking about this force that slows you down.

> Mechanical engineers create machines and devices that involve force and motion, such as cars, bicycles and roller coasters.

What a Drag!

As the engineers at Cervélo know, drag is, well, a real drag — they figure it accounts for 80 to 90 percent of the overall resistance affecting a rider . You might think that with those kinds of numbers stacked against you, there's not much you can do to improve your speed.

Fortunately, Cervélo engineers aren't daunted by numbers. The numbers just challenge them to create bike designs that reduce aerodynamic drag. But to cut down on drag, they first have to measure it.

Cervélo engineers measure drag in two ways:

1. *Computational fluid dynamics* allows them to test their designs virtually in a computer-simulated *wind tunnel* before going to the time and expense of building a prototype.

2. A low-speed wind tunnel allows them to simulate real-world conditions in a controlled environment.

Of course, it helps to have a low-speed wind tunnel on hand. Fortunately, Cervélo engineers do.

The name *Cervélo* comes from a combination of the Italian word for brain, *cervello*, and a French word for bike, *vélo*.

Extreme speed doesn't come cheap: a top-of-the-line Cervélo rolls out at $11 000.

KEY
DESIGN
STEP

Define

21

As a high school student, Sean McDermott, engineering director at Cervélo, enjoyed science class the most. So he decided to study engineering in university and eventually specialized in mechanical engineering because he loved its hands-on applications. While math and science skills are important, Sean says engineering can be a very creative career choice. For Sean, mechanical engineering is all about "creating products that meet needs that people may not even realize they have." Plus, he adds, "there is a lot of satisfaction in being able to ride something you created."

Testing, Testing, One, Two, Three ...

Low-speed wind tunnels are used for testing many things, such as skiing equipment, soccer balls and even aircraft and missiles! They can test at speeds up to 400 km/h (249 m.p.h.), but Cervélo engineers use them at about 48 km/h (30 m.p.h.) — an average race speed for competitive cyclists ✓. In the wind tunnel, fans blow air over the bike as it sits on a balance, which is like a scale. The balance measures forces such as lift (the force that keeps an airplane in the sky) and drag. All the data is recorded for later analysis.

A wind tunnel is only half the equation, though. To test a bike design, you need a rider: someone willing to sit in the same position ... on a bike ... in a wind tunnel ... all day long. Not surprisingly, a test rider is hard to find.

THE ENGINEER'S TOOLBOX

The engineer's toolbox is brimming with useful instruments and applications, from things that you probably have in your house — such as protractors and pliers — to sophisticated computer software. Many engineers use computer-aided design (CAD) software to make diagrams and create and test prototypes ⚙. Cervélo engineers, for example, use three-dimensional CAD software to improve their bike designs hundreds of times on the computer before they are built in real life 📈.

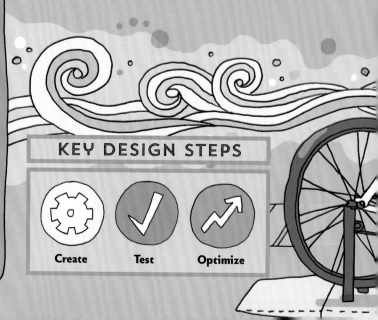

KEY DESIGN STEPS

Create   Test   Optimize

Dave Is No Dummy

Cervélo engineers eventually found their perfect test rider: Dave. He never gets tired, never gets hungry and never needs a bathroom break. That's because Dave is the world's first wind tunnel mannequin.

To make Dave, or Foam Dave as he's called at Cervélo, engineers first scanned U.S. champion cyclist Dave Zabriskie riding a bike in his aerodynamic position. Then they manufactured a life-sized copy of Dave out of high-density rigid foam. They use Foam Dave with a special bike skeleton, called a test mule. Engineers can quickly try a number of prototyped bike parts by bolting them to the steel test-mule frame, and just as easily unbolting them to swap in new parts. The combination of the ever-constant Foam Dave and the quick-change test mule allows Cervélo engineers to test their ideas one by one as they aim to reduce drag ✔.

It's a painstaking process. Sean McDermott, engineering director at Cervélo, says 8-hour tests at the wind tunnel can turn into 14-hour work days when factoring in time for setup and bike building. Using the test mule and Foam Dave, Cervélo engineers designed and tested over 157 different aerodynamic ideas while perfecting their P4 triathlon bike ⚡.

Engineered for Speed

Cervélo bikes have helped propel riders to victory in the Tour de France, Ironman World Championships and the Olympic Games. When Canadian cyclist Ryder Hesjedal won the 2012 Giro d'Italia, he was riding a Cervélo. The model he used, declared Cervélo, produces less drag than any other bicycle they have ever tested. Designing and building bicycles that help athletes go faster is what keeps Cervélo engineers — and Foam Dave — going. No wonder the company says, "Engineering is at the core of all we do."

Electrical Engineering

The Tyranny of Numbers

In 1946, a new device was unveiled to the public: the first practical electronic computer built in the United States. Newspapers called it an amazing machine and a wonder brain that held great possibilities for humankind. Among other functions, it could add and subtract 5000 times per second — a thousand times faster than any other machine at the time! Although the machine received massive praise, it was also just plain massive. If complex electronic equipment was going to be practical, it had to get smaller — much smaller. It took over a decade, but a newly hired electrical engineer developed the technology that would revolutionize the electronics industry.

Electrical engineers create devices that run on electricity, such as cell phones, televisions and robots. They can also develop wireless technology and maintain power systems.

ENIAC took up an entire room, but today the world's smallest computer is so tiny that nearly 150 of them can fit into a thimble!

Bigger Isn't Always Better

Designed during the Second World War, this early computer was called ENIAC (Electronic Numerical Integrator And Computer). It was built to help artillerymen fighting in the war calculate where their shells would fall. A shell trajectory calculation that could take someone three days to finish took ENIAC just 20 seconds! The downside? ENIAC took up a 9 x 15 m (30 x 50 ft.) room and weighed 27 000 kg (60 000 lb.) — that's the weight of a humpback whale! This whale of a computer was a far cry from today's tablets!

ENIAC contained thousands of parts, including almost 18 000 vacuum tubes, used to control the flow of electricity. The vacuum tubes were made of glass, which meant they were fragile. They were also big, produced a lot of heat and burned out. It didn't take a computer to figure it out: complex electronic equipment like ENIAC required too many parts ❶. Even the invention of the transistor in 1947, which did away with all those pesky vacuum tubes, didn't solve the problem. Electronic circuits (components such as resistors, capacitors and transistors connected together to perform different tasks) still required a lot of parts. And all of those parts needed to be connected by hand, each connection a potential failure point. This problem, dubbed the *"tyranny of numbers,"* came down to the fact that the components in electronic equipment had to be made smaller, lighter, less costly and more reliable ❷.

The ability to add and subtract at 5000 times per second may sound fast, but today's smartphones can handle over a trillion instructions per second!

KEY DESIGN STEPS

❗ **Define**   🔍 **Investigate**

TALENTED TEAM

With so many men away fighting during the Second World War, women were often recruited to do jobs traditionally held by men. They never received a lot of attention or fame, but a team of six women was responsible for programming ENIAC's shell trajectory calculations. Back then, there were no such things as programming languages or tools, so they programmed ENIAC by hand, physically plugging in wires and setting switches. It was challenging work, but these women knew ENIAC inside and out. They even came up with a system to figure out which one of the almost 18 000 vacuum tubes had burned out!

All Work and No Play

Enter Jack Kilby, a newly hired electrical engineer at Texas Instruments in Dallas. Jack had years of experience in experimenting with how to shrink and simplify electronic devices. But as the new kid on the block, he hadn't earned any vacation time. So when most of his coworkers were out of the office for a two-week summer break, Jack was in the lab, trying to figure out how to make electronic circuits smaller.

Jack realized that one of the major problems was that there were just too many materials being used to make the circuit's parts. His solution: make all the parts with a single material so they could be integrated (or combined) in a single chip 💡. No, not the sour cream and onion kind — Jack's chip was made from an element called germanium. This was the key to forming the smaller, simpler electronic circuit that would become known as an *integrated circuit*.

KEY DESIGN STEPS

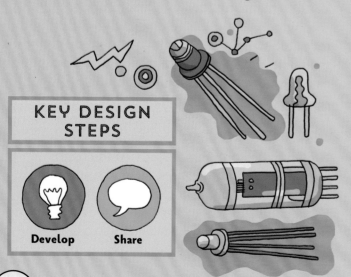

Develop   Share

ENGINEERING OVERLAP

There are many fields of engineering: agricultural, chemical, civil, computer, electrical, mechanical and structural, to name just a few. Sometimes the boundaries between these fields are not very strict. Electrical engineering, for example, overlaps with computer engineering since computers are electronic devices. But computer engineering is its own field because it focuses on everything computer, like hardware and software design.

The integrated circuit Jack showed his bosses in September 1958 was a thin chip of germanium, about half the size of a small paper clip, glued to a glass slide ⬭. With protruding wires and metal tabs, it wasn't going to win any beauty contests. But despite the unpolished look, when Jack turned on the power, it worked!

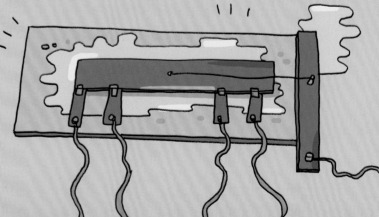

To the Moon and Beyond

The integrated circuit wasn't an overnight success. In fact, it wasn't until integrated circuits were used in the 1960s for programs like NASA's Project Apollo, which landed the first humans on the moon, that the technology started to really get noticed. To help popularize the technology, Jack also developed a more down-to-earth use for integrated circuits: the first handheld electronic calculator. While the early models were astronomically expensive — up to $500 for a calculator that today might sell for $5 — they showed the everyday potential for electronic equipment.

Today, integrated circuits are, well, an integral part of electronic devices, from computers to televisions to cell phones. In 2000, Jack was awarded the Nobel Prize in Physics for his part in inventing the integrated circuit — which probably made up for missing that summer vacation.

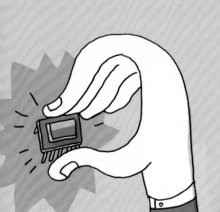

Team Member Bio

Electrical engineer Jack Kilby grew up in Great Bend, Kansas, where his father owned a small electric company. When Jack was in high school, an ice storm knocked down a lot of telephone and electric power lines. His dad worked with amateur radio operators to get in touch with his customers in rural Kansas, who had lost service. To Jack, amateur radio seemed fascinating. He said, "It sparked my interest in electronics, and that's when I decided that this field was something I wanted to pursue." Many years later, after winning the Nobel Prize, Jack wrote that electrical engineering still holds as many opportunities as when he was a college student: "My advice is to get involved and get started."

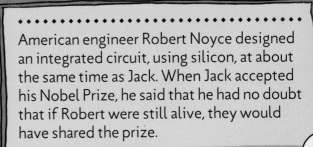

American engineer Robert Noyce designed an integrated circuit, using silicon, at about the same time as Jack. When Jack accepted his Nobel Prize, he said that he had no doubt that if Robert were still alive, they would have shared the prize.

Engineering above the Clouds

Summer vacation had finally arrived! In the south of France, huge numbers of people were heading down the A75 highway to sunbathe and splash on the beautiful Mediterranean coast.

That is, until traffic came to a screeching halt. The cause: a major bottleneck near the medieval town of Millau. While the traffic jams — sometimes *five hours long* — were a temporary headache for tourists, for the people of Millau, they were a perpetual nightmare. Something had to be done, so a French engineer conceived of a crazy plan to move the cars out of the valley and above the clouds.

Allons-y!

My donkey moves faster than this!

KEY DESIGN STEP

Define

Civil engineers create structures such as bridges, skyscrapers, roads, tunnels and dams.

28

That Tarn Valley

The source of all this automotive angst was the Tarn Valley, a 2.5 km (1.6 mi.) wide gorge where the Tarn River runs between two tall plateaus. When the A75 highway was originally built, no one knew quite what to do about the Tarn Valley, so they basically ignored it, building the highway to the edge of the gorge and then continuing it again on the other side. Cars traveling along the A75 had to go down into the town of Millau, cross the Tarn River on a small bridge, climb up the other side of the valley and then finally get back on the highway ❶. Needless to say, Millau was not built for that kind of traffic, since the town was founded long before cars were even invented!

BIG BUILDS

Engineering megaprojects like the Burj Khalifa, the tallest building in the world, are usually billed as civil engineering projects. But it takes a team of many engineering specialists — including geotechnical, structural and environmental engineers — to make these big builds a big success.

29

You Say *Bouchon*, I Say Traffic Jam

Everyone was sick and tired of the infamous *bouchon de Millau*. The perpetual traffic jam, or *bouchon* in French, was a huge pain in the butt for everyone involved: tourists, townsfolk, the mayor of Millau and French officials.

Everyone agreed they had a big challenge: they had to fill in the missing link in the A75 so travelers would not have to leave the highway and detour down into Millau to cross the river. They also agreed that the solution to the problem, whatever it might be, had to provide access to Millau and attract more tourists to the area — and it had to look good, too 🔍!

NIMBY

By 1987, officials had decided to do something about the A75. Engineers were then faced with deciding exactly where to put the new route — and that's when many residents of the area came down with a serious case of *NIMBY (Not In My Back Yard)*. While everyone agreed that they needed a solution, most residents also agreed they didn't want the new highway slicing through their picturesque French town 🔍.

Four routes were suggested and compared 🔍. While the routes varied in length, cost and location, they all had one thing in common: decidedly unimaginative names.

1. The *grand est* (great east) route would go east of Millau, with two long bridges crossing the Tarn and Dourbie Valleys. This would allow people to drive through the region quickly, but did not meet the criterion of ensuring good access to Millau. Plus, residents of the Dourbie Valley caught the case of NIMBY that was going around, not wanting the highway in their "backyards."

2. The *grand ouest* (great west) option would bypass Millau to the west. Unfortunately, it was also a victim of NIMBY, as it would mean passing through the Cernon Valley and its pretty villages. It also failed to meet the criterion of providing good access to Millau.

3. The *proche de la RN9* (near the RN9) would mean good access to Millau, but it had some technical difficulties to overcome and would have to include a steep downhill slope that could be dangerous for trucks.

4. The *médiane* (median, or midpoint) route would bypass Millau to the west, relieving the traffic and noise problems, but still provide an easy way to access the town. The geology of the Tarn Valley — with limestone that was challenging to build on — was an issue with this plan, but experts decided it was workable.

Finally, on June 28, 1989, the fourth route was chosen — but that only led to more options that had to be weighed.

The High Way

The first option was to go high, building a 2.5 km (1.6 mi.) *viaduct* (a type of bridge) above the Tarn River. The second option was to go low, bypassing the town by going down into the valley, crossing the river with a new bridge and building a 2.3 km (1.4 mi.) viaduct and a tunnel up the other side.

Again, the possible solutions were compared 💡. The low solution came out on the bottom: it was going to cost more, increase driving times and affect the local water table.

On October 29, 1991, French officials decided to go with the high way for the new highway. With that decision behind them, they held a design competition to decide what kind of bridge they would build.

KEY DESIGN STEPS

Investigate   Develop

A Man with a (Crazy) Plan

Michel Virlogeux, an engineer who had been involved with the project, knew what kind of bridge he would build. He wanted something that fit the quiet, natural surroundings.

He had sketched out a design for an elegant bridge that would soar high across the Tarn Valley. His *cable-stayed bridge* would feature long cables attached to tall towers that would support the weight of the bridge's deck, or road 💡.

A cable-stayed bridge was a daring plan — suspension bridges (a different kind of cable bridge) were a more common choice for spanning such long distances. But Michel wouldn't give up on his bridge. He quit his job with the French highway administration so that he could officially enter the design competition. Working with English architect Lord Norman Foster, he improved his original design 📈. All their hard work paid off — their design solution was a winner!

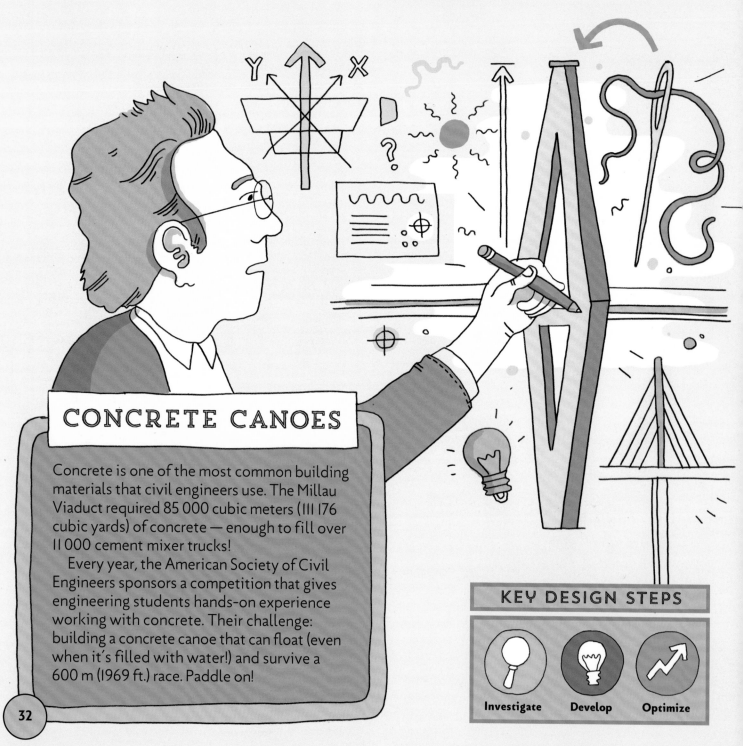

CONCRETE CANOES

Concrete is one of the most common building materials that civil engineers use. The Millau Viaduct required 85 000 cubic meters (111 176 cubic yards) of concrete — enough to fill over 11 000 cement mixer trucks!

Every year, the American Society of Civil Engineers sponsors a competition that gives engineering students hands-on experience working with concrete. Their challenge: building a concrete canoe that can float (even when it's filled with water!) and survive a 600 m (1969 ft.) race. Paddle on!

KEY DESIGN STEPS

Investigate   Develop   Optimize

Vive le Viaduc!

The bridge's construction could finally begin, with a few additional requirements: the bridge must be built to last for 120 years and it must be finished on time and on budget 🕐. It was a tall order — for a tall bridge. And while it took a glacially slow 14 years from the first discussions in 1987 to the start of construction in 2001, the bridge — officially called the Viaduc de Millau (Millau Viaduct) — was actually built in only three years.

On a cloudy day, the delicate structure appears to float above the valley. Impressive, for sure.

But how well did the Millau Viaduct fulfill its main design specifications?

- ✔ Filled in the missing link in the A75.
- ✔ Provided access to Millau.
- ✔ Finished on time.
- ✔ Finished on budget.
- ✔✔ Pleasing to look at. (Check and double check!)

In fact, the bridge has increased tourism by becoming a local attraction itself. Plus, it satisfies both residents and tourists — and has people pulling out their cameras, not their hair!

Soaring high above the clouds, the Millau Viaduct is the tallest bridge in the world! Its highest point measures 343 m (1125 ft.) — that's taller than the Eiffel Tower. It is even visible from space!

Geomatics Engineering

Not-So-At-Home on the Range

In some video games, you get three lives before it's game over. In real life, though, you only get one. Time is running out for the woodland caribou herd of Alberta's Little Smoky range. About 95 percent of their habitat has been disturbed by logging and oil and gas extraction, and the herd is at risk of extinction. With the human world closing in on the caribou, a professor of geomatics engineering collaborated on a project to create a virtual environment that might help give the herd a fighting chance.

Geomatics engineers use location technology, such as *GPS* and Google Earth, to create ways to observe, monitor and predict things that happen on our planet.

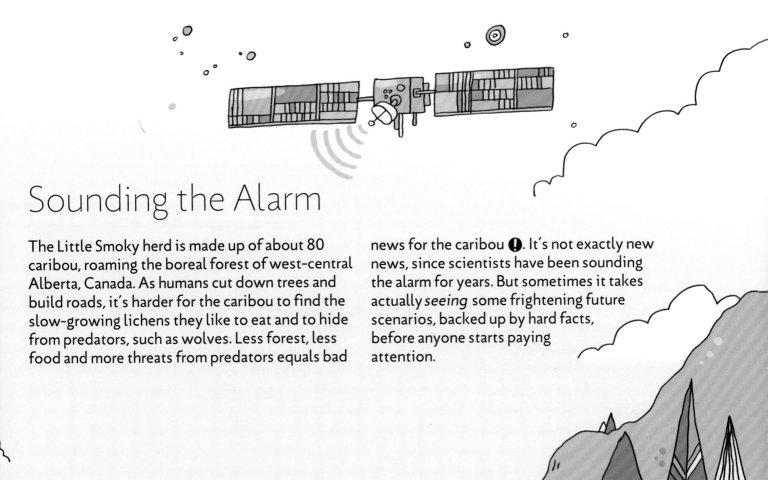

Sounding the Alarm

The Little Smoky herd is made up of about 80 caribou, roaming the boreal forest of west-central Alberta, Canada. As humans cut down trees and build roads, it's harder for the caribou to find the slow-growing lichens they like to eat and to hide from predators, such as wolves. Less forest, less food and more threats from predators equals bad news for the caribou ❶. It's not exactly new news, since scientists have been sounding the alarm for years. But sometimes it takes actually *seeing* some frightening future scenarios, backed up by hard facts, before anyone starts paying attention.

KEY
DESIGN
STEP

❶
Define

You Are Here

Geomatics was the key to predicting those future scenarios. "You might not know what geomatics stands for, but many people use it almost every day," says Dr. Danielle Marceau, a geomatics engineering professor at the University of Calgary in Alberta. You're using geomatics when you use a maps app to find your friend's house or GPS to go hiking with your family.

Danielle was part of a team that used geomatics and a computer design program to create a virtual environment (or model) to understand how industries such as logging and oil are affecting the Little Smoky caribou. Building the model took a lot of data — and almost a year of work. Remote sensing imagery (think satellite imagery) was used to create a special map, called a *land cover map*. It showed what covers the land (such as forest, water or grass) where the caribou live. The map included industrial features such as roads, pipelines and oil wells. Of course, the virtual environment also included information about the caribou, such as how much food they need, how fast they move and where 13 real female caribou wearing GPS collars were located.

GEOMATICS: WHERE IT'S AT!

A new generation of engineers is learning about pressing environmental problems — and figuring out how to solve them — using geomatics. These engineers monitor climate change, predict floods and study how animals adapt to changing environments. They also model ways to reduce deforestation and investigate how cities can grow sustainably. A relatively new, but growing field, geomatics is where it's at!

KEY DESIGN STEP

Share

Sim Caribou

When finished, the model was used to realistically simulate caribou behavior and movement. The research team found that industrial features, such as roads and pipelines, not only decrease the caribou's habitat and food sources, but they influence their movement and their energy levels. Danielle explains that "caribou react to industrial features in their habitat. They perceive industrial features as being high risk, and they avoid them." This creates a "landscape of fear," Danielle says, even when predators aren't around.

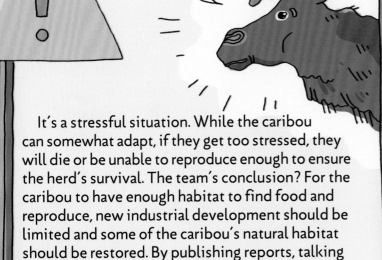

It's a stressful situation. While the caribou can somewhat adapt, if they get too stressed, they will die or be unable to reproduce enough to ensure the herd's survival. The team's conclusion? For the caribou to have enough habitat to find food and reproduce, new industrial development should be limited and some of the caribou's natural habitat should be restored. By publishing reports, talking at conferences and showing their results to the government, Danielle and her team are ensuring their message gets heard — for the future of the Little Smoky herd ◯.

THE EIGHTH WONDER OF THE WORLD

GPS technology is used in many engineering projects — it has even been used to create an island! Located off the coast of Dubai in the Persian Gulf, Palm Jumeirah is part of an engineering project dubbed "The Eighth Wonder of the World." The artificial island, built from sand in the shape of a palm tree, is one of the world's largest human-made islands. During the five-year megaproject, dredging ships scooped up enough sand to fill over 37 000 Olympic-sized swimming pools. Engineers used enhanced GPS technology to distribute the sand to within 1 cm (3/8 in.) of where they wanted it — now *that's* precise!

The Wonderful Wizard of Woz

Life was pretty rough back when your grandparents were kids. They had to walk to and from school — uphill both ways, of course — and they didn't have cell phones, tablets or personal computers. Just imagine: to research school projects, they could only use books!

Wikipedia wasn't even a glimmer in a programmer's eye. The computers that did exist were enormous in size — and in price. One Californian kid was dreaming big, though — dreaming of a day when computers would be as common as ... apples. (Hint, hint!)

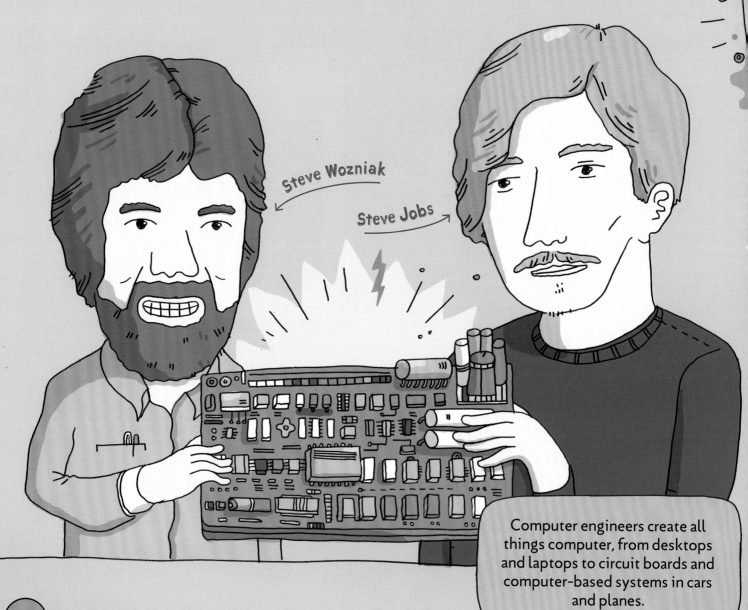

Steve Wozniak

Steve Jobs

Computer engineers create all things computer, from desktops and laptops to circuit boards and computer-based systems in cars and planes.

Cream Soda Computer

When Steve Wozniak was a high school student in the 1960s, he dreamed of the day when anyone could buy a computer, take it home and learn how to use it. Steve (whose nickname is "Woz") got tired of waiting for it to happen, so he started designing his own computers — on paper because he couldn't afford the parts ! He designed them over and over again, aiming to use the fewest parts possible. Fewer parts meant the computers would be less costly to build and easier to fix if anything went wrong.

A few years later, an executive at a computer company gave Steve about 20 chips, and he and a friend built a computer together. It was very basic, but it could run a simple program. Their favorite beverage inspired the name: the Cream Soda Computer. Steve's next computer would also be named after something delicious.

Knock, knock.

Along with his computer skills, Steve is known for loving a good laugh. In the early 1970s, he started a Dial-a-Joke phone service that got up to 2000 calls a day!

KEY DESIGN STEPS

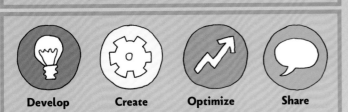

Develop   Create   Optimize   Share

Apples to Apples

By 1975, Steve had a job designing calculators, but in his spare time, he started working on another computer. As always, his goal was to use the fewest parts possible. That computer would be called the Apple I.

Steve Wozniak's friend Steve Jobs thought they should start a company to sell the Apple I. They advertised it as being essentially "hassle free." They said your system could be up and running in minutes. Add a keyboard and a monitor, and you had yourself a compact, desktop computer that could develop programs and play games, among other functions.

It took one more computer, the Apple II, to really start a revolution. Steve explained that "a personal computer should be small, reliable, convenient to use and inexpensive." Introduced in 1977, the Apple II — featuring a keyboard, built-in programming language and color graphics — was all that and more. Finally, here was a computer that many people could afford, take home and use. Steve's childhood dream was now a reality.

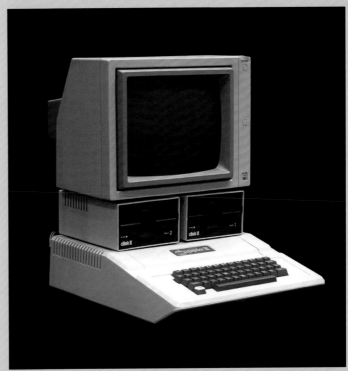

The Apple II, pictured here with floppy disk drives and a monitor, launched a computer revolution. Steve called it the first low-cost computer you didn't have to be a geek to use.

39

When Good Sewers Go Bad

Nestled near the Willamette River, close to Portland, Oregon, is the beautiful city of Lake Oswego. It has quaint shops, picturesque parks and, of course, a lovely lake that is surrounded by equally lovely homes. But, not so long ago, the city also had a rather, *ahem*, indelicate problem. There's just no polite way to say this: the problem was poop. And no, it wasn't just a poopy problem, the problem was poop itself! Lurking beneath the calm surface of Oswego Lake lay a disaster just waiting to happen, and it was up to environmental engineers to fix it.

> Environmental engineers create ways to keep the planet clean by controlling pollution, finding new recycling methods and harnessing renewable energy from the sun and wind.

WASTE WATER

A Sticky Situation

Built in the early 1960s, Lake Oswego's aging sewer system (part of which ran through the lake) was no longer up to the task of flushing away wastewater for a population of 37 000. Something had to give — and it did.

You know that old joke: what's brown and sticky? (Answer: a stick.) Well, let's just say that in Lake Oswego, the answer was *not* a stick. During a heavy rainfall, the system backed up and sewage flowed into the lake — a popular place for kayaking, boating and swimming. *Pee-yew!*

To make matters worse, the sewer's steel supports were corroding. Engineers concluded that even a moderate earthquake could cause severe breaks in the pipeline and send millions of liters, or gallons, of raw sewage spilling into the lake ❗. Lake Oswego could soon become Lake Os-We-Don't-Go!

KEY
DESIGN
STEP

❗

Define

41

Making a (Long!) List

Clearly, the sewer system would have to be replaced. The endeavor got under way like many public works projects: slowly, with years of planning, community briefings and engineering studies to determine the new system's requirements.

It was agreed that the new sewer system must solve the old system's capacity and structural problems, last for at least 75 years, withstand a moderate earthquake with no damage and be repairable after a major quake. The system also had to be operated and maintained safely and affordably 🔦.

There was also a long list of constraints to consider: the topography of the land around the lake (steep bluffs and hills) and the geology of the lake bottom (soft sediment) made building the sewer system a challenge, private property around the lake limited construction access and lake temperatures varied up to 22°C (35°F) between summer and winter, which could affect building materials 🔦. *Whew!* The list of criteria and constraints was almost as long as the 4 km (2.5 mi.) lake itself.

TEAM S.A.V.E.

Five seventh-graders created a video game about LOIS. Calling themselves team SAVE (Super Awesome Video game Engineers), they won second prize in the Oregon Game Programming Challenge. In the video game, players have to fix the sewer system before they run out of oxygen or before pollution reaches overload. They also have to watch out for suckerfish and lamprey eels!

PRIVATE PROPERTY

KEY DESIGN STEPS

Investigate

Develop

Investigating the Ins and Outs

Multiple solutions for the new sewer system, called LOIS (Lake Oswego Interceptor Sewer), were considered, and two main contenders emerged 🔍.

1. The around-the-lake option would mean constructing six large pump stations on private property throughout the community to pump water from lower to higher elevations. This option would also disrupt the whole city, since it would mean constructing another 6.4 km (4 mi.) of sewer pipes below its busy streets. Plus, operating and maintaining the pump stations would add a significant cost — $20 million — to the project.

2. The in-lake option would rebuild the sewer in the lake using a *buoyant gravity sewer*. The new, more durable design would include a buoyant, or floating, pipeline that used gravity, not expensive pumping stations, to move sewage through the system. The sewer would be less costly to build and maintain than the other option and would meet the criterion of being earthquake resistant.

Finally, in 2007, the city council decided the in-lake option was the way to go. The system they chose would become the world's first buoyant gravity sewer — and it was the result of a flash of engineering inspiration.

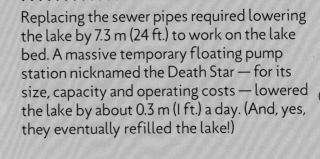

Replacing the sewer pipes required lowering the lake by 7.3 m (24 ft.) to work on the lake bed. A massive temporary floating pump station nicknamed the Death Star — for its size, capacity and operating costs — lowered the lake by about 0.3 m (1 ft.) a day. (And, yes, they eventually refilled the lake!)

STICKS-IN-THE-MUD

When the new LOIS system was being built, several people got stuck in the exposed lake bed mud. So firefighters started practicing rescue drills on the muddy lake bed using an inflatable sled, designed for water and snow, in case there were any more sticks-in-the-mud.

Two Heads Are Better than One

Environmental engineer Jon Holland was a member of the large team of engineers and contractors who worked on the project. He developed the idea for the buoyant gravity sewer after thinking, *Wouldn't it be cool if we could hang the pipe from a float on the surface of the lake* 💡*?* That would do away with having to use expensive non-corrosive supports coming up from the lake bed. But Jon knew a large float would interfere with boating and other activities on the lake's surface.

This artist's drawing shows off some of LOIS's best features: the submerged pipeline, wire rope tethers and the twin buoyancy pipes that help keep the pipeline in position. Even the fish seem happy with this ingenious solution!

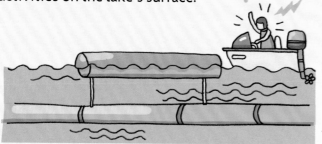

Jon shared his problem with a coworker, who suggested, "Why not make the pipe buoyant and use anchors to hold it down at the right level beneath the surface?" This would keep the lake's surface free and clear. Jon knew they had found the answer!

The pipeline, made of strong high-density polyethylene plastic, is held underwater by stainless steel wire rope tethers fastened to anchor bars drilled into bedrock below the lake. Smaller twin buoyancy pipes filled with air are attached to the pipeline to provide the buoyant force needed to keep the tethers taut. Installing the pipe in a curvy S-shape limits sideways movement when the pipe expands in warmer water and contracts in cooler water. The pipe is also flexible enough to withstand an earthquake. Keeping the pipe positioned at a gradual downward slope means the system doesn't need to be pumped, since gravity forces unmentionables through the pipe all the way to the treatment plant.

KEY DESIGN STEPS

Develop   **Share**

The Sweetest Smell

The successful completion of the $95 million project — on time *and* under budget — was not the end of the story, though. The LOIS project has won a dozen awards, including the 2012 grand prize in the design category from the American Academy of Environmental Engineers and Scientists. There's been worldwide interest in the project, too. Jon says, "We've been to Washington, DC; Vancouver, BC; and Beijing, China — as well as many other cities throughout the U.S. — to speak about this unusual project"○.

Team Member Bio

Jon Holland, team leader for the LOIS project, always liked solving math and science problems. But Jon says engineering isn't just thinking about what can be done, but also about what should be done. He chose to become an environmental engineer because it satisfies his idealistic make-a-difference side. "If we foul our nest, what then?" he asks. "Better to wake up and take care of our home." The LOIS project challenged Jon to do just that, by protecting the lake's habitat with a reliable new sewer system.

The real winners, of course, are the residents of Lake Oswego. At the end of the day, the only thing wafting through their city, even after a heavy rain, is the sweet smell of success!

45

Glossary

aerospace engineering: the field of engineering that deals with the design, development and testing of aircraft and spacecraft

alkaline battery: a common battery type that creates electricity from a chemical reaction between manganese dioxide and zinc

biomedical engineering: the field of engineering that solves problems relating to human health

bioprinter: a device using 3D printing technology to create human tissue by building layer upon layer of living cells

buoyant gravity sewer: a system in which gravity and a buoyant pipeline, held underwater by flexible wire tethers and anchors, move sewage to a treatment plant

cable-stayed bridge: a type of bridge in which long cables attached to tall towers support the weight of the bridge's deck, or road

chemical engineering: the field of engineering that involves the production and use of chemicals to create a wide variety of products, including foods and fuels

civil engineering: the field of engineering that deals with the design, construction and maintenance of structures such as roads and bridges

computational fluid dynamics: the use of computer programs to analyze and solve problems relating to the way fluids (liquids and gases) move

computer engineering: the field of engineering that deals with designing and developing computers and computer-based systems

constraint: in engineering, the restrictions or limitations placed on a design, often relating to cost, time and available materials

criteria: in engineering, the desired features or qualities of a design

drag: a force that opposes an object's motion through a fluid (liquid or gas)

electrical engineering: the field of engineering that deals with designing and building devices that run on electricity

engineer: a person who finds solutions to problems by improving existing technology and developing new technology

engineering: a profession that uses mathematics and science knowledge to design solutions to problems

environmental engineering: the field of engineering that develops ways to improve the quality of air, land and water

geomatics engineering: the field of engineering that uses location technology, such as GPS, to observe and predict things that happen on Earth. *See also* GPS (global positioning system).

GPS (global positioning system): a navigation system that gives people with ground receivers their location, based on signals from orbiting satellites

integrated circuit: an electronic circuit of multiple components (such as resistors and capacitors) constructed on a single chip

Mars Science Laboratory (MSL): a NASA mission that successfully landed the rover *Curiosity* on the surface of Mars in August 2012

mechanical engineering: the field of engineering that designs, builds and maintains mechanical devices (ones that involve force and motion)

NIMBY (Not In My Back Yard): opposition to a new development by the neighborhood's residents

prototype: a working model that allows engineers to test their design in the real world

Sky Crane maneuver: a landing system that used nylon tethers to safely lower the *Curiosity* rover to a soft landing on the surface of Mars

tyranny of numbers: recognized in the 1950s, a problem resulting from the fact that complex electronic equipment required too many components to be practical

viaduct: a long, high bridge, made up of a series of spans, that supports a road or railway across a valley or other obstacle

wind tunnel: a tunnel-like structure in which powerful fans blow air past an object to analyze its aerodynamics

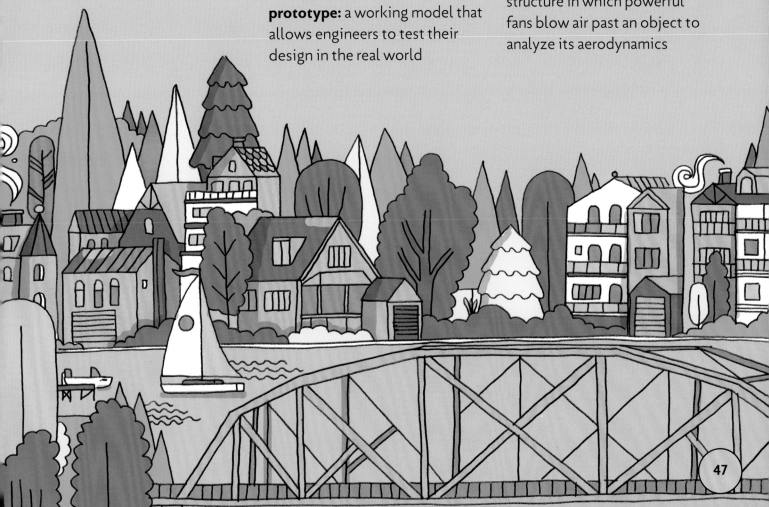

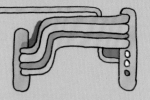

Index